M000094375

Top of the First

The Convergence of Heath Care and Financial Planning

Peter Stahl

2018 Edition

Copyright © Bedrock Business Results LLC 2018

All rights reserved. No part of this publication may be reproduced, stored in a retrieval system, or transmitted, in any form, or by any means, electronic, mechanical, photocopying, recording, or otherwise, without the prior consent of the publisher.

Sale of this book without a front cover may be unauthorized. If the book is coverless, it may have been reported to the publisher as "unsold or destroyed" and neither the author nor the publisher may have received payment for it.

The information may reference Medicare, Medicaid, Social Security, tax and/ or legal issues but such materials are not intended to provide tax, legal and or accounting advice. As with all matters of a legal nature, you should consult your tax or legal counsel for advice. The information is provided as a general overview. It is derived from the Internal Revenue Code, Medicare.gov and other government publications, all subject matter sources reasonably believed to be reliable. Tax law and the laws governing Medicare/Medicaid are complex and subject to change. Clients should consult with their attorney and/or qualified tax advisor when making decisions regarding these matters.

Table of Contents

Introduction

"It's getting late early" — Yogi Berra

The task of planning and preparing for your retirement years has many components. One of these components, health care, has risen to the forefront of major issues facing our nation. As I speak to individuals and financial advisors about the impact of health care costs on their retirement income plans, it is obvious that most people are just beginning to recognize the need to incorporate health care planning into their financial planning. As they say in baseball, we are in the top of the first inning. Common wisdom encourages us to begin any financial planning process early allowing time for the plan to work. In this respect, the top of the first inning is a good place to be. The challenge we face as a nation is that the front edge of the largest segment of the U.S. population is already entering their retirement years. As Yogi Berra, might say, "It's getting late early."

There is an abundance of information available regarding how to effectively save and invest your money in order to build a source of income for that period of time following your chosen career. This involves decisions such as the type of investment products you should own and optimal allocations within equity, fixed income, domestic, international, growth, and value. These are critical decisions but most of the planning process, until recently, has failed to incorporate the impact of health care costs. Those heading into retirement have communicated that these costs represent one of their largest concerns. This is quite understandable.

- The age 50+ population ranks health care expenses as their top financial concern for retirement.[1]

- This same group states that the information needed to determine health care costs is overwhelming, confusing, and frustrating.[2]

I do not wish to bombard the reader with statistics, but rather to point out that the concerns are justified. Simply put, Americans are living much longer lives in a country that enjoys some of the finest medical care available anywhere in the world. This care is expensive. Diligent planning and saving for these expenditures need to take place. Most of the popular media describes how Americans are not financially prepared for retirement. There are, however, at least some encouraging trends.

- 45% of workers age 50-64 (peak retirement savings years) are saving specifically for health care costs. This percentage has doubled over the last six years.[3]

Recognizing the need to plan for this cost is a solid start, but exactly how you choose to plan and invest for these expenditures will determine how effective these investments will be in funding your health care expenditures.

The purpose of this book is to provide those who are saving and investing for retirement, as well as those already in retirement, strategies to ensure that your investment planning incorporates the optimal strategies to provide for health care expenses. Medicare, the mandatory means most Americans will utilize for retirement health care insurance, will play a major role in this discussion. Medicare costs and the taxation of Medicare premiums have a direct impact on retirement income. There are tangible, immediate steps you can take to make sure you are financially prepared.

Proper financial planning contributes to peace of mind. Given the enormity of health care costs, these strategies have a meaningful impact on your ability to create efficient sources of retirement income, meet your health care expenses, and feel secure in your retirement.

Once again, the focus is on the convergence of financial planning and health care costs. Although I will provide an overview of various elements of your health care coverage, this book is not a resource manual for the details of Medicare, Medigap polices, or custodial care. Speaking about the convergence of financial planning with health care, the content is naturally most beneficial to those who are investing for retirement or those who are in retirement, having accumulated some level of wealth to provide for their expenses. In fact, larger levels of assets usually equate to increased taxation and higher Medicare premiums. The more diligent you are with investing, the greater the benefit these strategies will be.

As we move into 2018, there is potential for change in our nation's health care system. It is important to recognize that health care can be generally divided into two phases. The first is health care provision during working years, with most insurance being coordinated by employers and through the government health care exchanges. Most of the immediate proposals for change will center on this phase of coverage.

The second phase is health care during retirement, with Medicare as the primary means of coverage. *Top of the First* is focused on this second phase, with much of the preparation taking place during working years. The most recent Medicare Trustee report forecasts a fiscal shortfall in 2029, with revenues insufficient to meet expenditures, unless the program is reformed.[4] I hope 2018 is the year when tangible steps are taken to begin this challenging but much needed process. Whether or not improvements are implemented, much of the program, including means testing for premium prices, the importance of estimating costs, and the value of accumulating sources of tax free income, will remain intact. The recommendations put forward in this book, therefore, will remain applicable.

Certain biases will become evident as you read this material. The most obvious one I will state up front. You will find multiple references to financial advisors and the need to work with your advisor to implement the strategies described in this book. Comprehensive financial planning is complex, especially when including the nuances of health care costs and taxation. I believe that consolidating financial assets with a competent financial advisor, who will consult with your tax professional, is the most prudent way to tackle the task. There are those who have the interest, time, and knowledge to create and maintain these plans on their own, but in my experience, they represent a distinct minority.

My hope is that you will adopt these ideas early on as you invest and plan for retirement.

CHAPTER 1

An Overview of Medicare

"Baseball is like church. Many attend, few understand."—Leo Durocher (US baseball manager, 1906-1991)

There are four questions that need to be answered in order to obtain the financial peace we desire as it relates to the daunting cost of health care in retirement.

1. Who provides health insurance coverage for this stage of life?

2. How does the coverage work?

3. How much will health expenditures cost?

4. How do I best financially prepare?

I address the first two questions in this chapter. The place to begin, therefore, in planning for health care in retirement is to gain a basic understanding of Medicare. Many are enrolled in Medicare but few understand it well. As it stands today, Medicare will be the method of insurance for most Americans during retirement. It is the federal health insurance program for people who are 65 or older. Some individuals will have employer provided insurance to supplement their Medicare, others (veterans, for example) may have Medicare supplemented by insurance provided by groups like TriCare. Whether you have ancillary coverage or not, Medicare will be a meaningful part of your future. I will provide an overview of the alphabet soup that comprises Medicare, as well as an explanation of how the pieces are put together to form the two most common coverage plans. Summaries are provided throughout the chapters, highlighting the most important information tied to your investment planning. The purpose is not to describe the minutia, eligibility and coverage of Medicare (one source of that detail is Medicare.gov), but to become reasonably fluent with the various parts in order to understand the impact on your financial plan.

We will begin our overview of Medicare with a description of the most common coverage plan: Original Medicare (Parts A & B) with a Medigap policy and prescription drug policy (Part D).

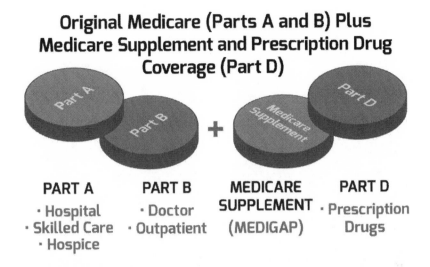

Original Medicare (Parts A and B) Plus Medicare Supplement and Prescription Drug Coverage (Part D)

PART A	PART B	MEDICARE SUPPLEMENT (MEDIGAP)	PART D
· Hospital	· Doctor		· Prescription
· Skilled Care	· Outpatient		Drugs
· Hospice			

2018 Medicare Part A[5]

Medicare Part A primarily covers three services:

1. Hospital Coverage:

- Days 1-60: full coverage

- Days 61-90: you pay $335 per day coinsurance

- Days 91+: you pay $670 per day coinsurance while using 60 lifetime reserve days

2. Skilled Nursing Facility (for a qualified stay):

- Days 1-20: full coverage

- Days 21-100: you pay $167.50 daily deductible

- Days 101+: no coverage

3. Hospice Care:

- Care one receives in the final stage of life: full coverage

Part A does have a deductible ($1,340 per benefit period) for year 2018. It is important to note that this deductible, as well as some of the coinsurance listed above can be covered under a "Medigap" plan, which will be described later in this chapter.

Medicare Part A receives its funding from a couple of sources. The first source is a payroll tax of 2.9%. The employee and the employer split the tax evenly each paying 1.45%. Beginning in 2014, the Patient Protection Affordable Care Act introduced two additional taxes for couples earning over $250,000 or single filers earning over $200,000. The first is an added .9% tax on earned income. The second is a 3.8% tax on net investment income.[6] If your income is close to these levels, discuss this tax with your financial advisor and tax professional. If you are able to manage income flows, capital gains, and utilize tax favored investments to keep you below these income thresholds, the tax savings are meaningful.

Since the funding for Part A is provided by the aforementioned taxes, most people will not pay anything for this insurance coverage when they enroll at retirement. The general rule is that this coverage is free if you or your spouse have paid Social Security and Medicare taxes for at least ten years. If you are not eligible for free Part A coverage, the premium can cost up to $5,064 per year.⁷ Most people are eligible and enroll in Medicare Part A when they reach age 65. There are special considerations for those who need Part A due to a disability prior to age 65. You may wish to delay your enrollment in Part A beyond age 65 if you have creditable coverage from an employer health insurance plan. This is most common when one desires to continue funding into a Health Savings Account. This strategy will be discussed in chapter 4. For a full description of enrollment and eligibility, visit Medicare.gov.

Medicare Part B[8]

Medicare Part B, your doctor and outpatient services coverage, handles two types of services.

- Medically necessary services: Services or supplies that are needed to diagnose or treat your medical condition and that meet accepted standards of medical practice.

- Preventive services: Health care to prevent illness (like the flu) or detect it at an early stage, when treatment is most likely to work best.

Medicare B has a $183 (2018) annual deductible, 20% coinsurance (with no limit), and a monthly premium based on your income.

Most people pay the Medicare Part B premium with a

deduction directly from their Social Security benefit. Since Medicare is now mandatory, this reduction from your retirement income stream can be delayed but is ultimately, unavoidable. The amount of your 2018 premium is based on your 2016 income (Modified Adjusted Gross Income) meaning "higher" income earners will have a substantially higher premium (see chart below). This is referred to as an Income Related Monthly Adjustment (IRMAA). To put it more plainly, it is a tax. Once again, the IRMAA tax is an extra charge added to your premium.

Determining Your Medicare Part B Premium

2016 Single Modified AGI	2016 Joint Modified AGI	2018 Annual Part B Premium
$85,000 or Less	Less than $170,000	$1,608
$85,001 - $107,000	$170,001 - $214,000	$2,250
$107,001 - $133,500	$214,001 - $267,000	$3,214
$133,501 - $160,000	$267,001 - $320,000	$4,179
Above $160,000	Above $320,000	$5,143

As the chart shows, individuals in the lowest income bracket now pay $1,608 per year for Part B coverage. It is actually a monthly premium, that most people have deducted from their Social Security Benefit.

There is a small percent of the population who pay less than the standard $1,608. The reason that cost varies within this first income bracket is somewhat complex. The short answer is that some individuals have been sheltered from some of the Medicare Part B cost increases over the past few years. Most of the sheltering disappeared in 2018 when the majority of those paying less than $1,608 saw their premium increase to this amount.

To fully understand what is occurring, there is a piece of legislation (2009 Hold Harmless Act) that provides relief for individuals who are in the lowest income IRMAA bracket. For those in this category, increases in Part B premiums cannot exceed the amount of a Social Security cost of living adjustment (COLA). Each October the Social Security Administration announces the cost of living adjustment for the following calendar year. Following that announcement, the Center for Medicare and Medicaid Services provides the cost adjustment for Medicare Part B premiums. This means that part B premium increases can eliminate some or all of a Social Security pay raise, but cannot decrease the benefit for those in the first IRMAA bracket. When Medicare Part B prices rise, new Medicare enrollees pay the full amount of any increase. The result is that enrollees into the Medicare system over the past couple of years had been paying a higher premium than enrollees from previous years. To provide some perspective:

- The 2016 Social Security COLA was 0% and the Medicare Part B increase was 16%.

- The 2017 Social Security COLA was .3% and the Medicare Part B increase was approximately 10%.

It is important to recognize that the inflation rate on Part B premiums has averaged over 7% since Medicare's inception in 1966.[9] This is well above the 1.0% to 2.0% cost of living adjustment we are accustomed to seeing on Social Security benefits. The combination of the IRMAA tax and rising Part B premiums could result in a flat or even steadily declining Social Security benefit for some retirees. Once again, there is a piece of legislation (2009 Hold Harmless Act) that provides relief for individuals in the lowest IRMAA bracket. For those in this category, increases in Part B premiums cannot exceed the amount of a Social Security cost of living increase. This means that Part B premium increases can eliminate some or all of a Social Security pay raise, but cannot decrease the benefit. Those in any of IRMAA bracket above the first, experience the full increase in Medicare Part B premiums each year.

Another important item to note is that the Social Security Administration considers your income from two years ago to determine your current Medicare premiums. If you experience a life changing event and a resulting drop in income, you may be able to lower your tax by having the administration consider your current income. In order to accomplish this, you can apply with a form (SSA-44) that is sent into the Social Security Administration. The most common acceptable reasons are loss of income due to retirement, death of a spouse, or divorce. The form is located at SocialSecurity.gov.

When examining the income levels that trigger Medicare taxation, there are important considerations. Medicare is under enormous financial strains. The 2017 trustee report forecasts that outflows will outpace funding by 2029 if no action is taken.[10] The Congressional Budget Office estimates that there are close to 56 million Americans covered by Medicare, a figure that will rise to approximately 70 million people in 2030 and 80 million in 2039. Only an estimated 5% of Americans are currently paying the Medicare tax, meaning their Modified Adjusted Gross Income is above $170,000 for a couple or above $85,000 for a single filer. It has been estimated that the number of people paying the IRMAA tax needs to increase to 20%-25% of the population as part of a plan to keep Medicare solvent. More taxpayers are gradually moving into higher tax brackets, as the brackets are not indexed for inflation (and cannot be until 2020). More drastic measures, however, are probable. For example, a bipartisan commission on health care reform recommended that the taxation begin at income levels of $90,000 for a couple and $60,000 for singles.[11]

In addition to the lowering of income levels that trigger taxation, there are also factors causing taxable incomes to rise. For example, on June 1, 2016 10,000 baby boomers turned age 70-1/2. This daily occurrence will continue for the next 18 years. Age 70-1/2 is when taxable, required minimum distributions begin on trillions of dollars of qualified IRA, 403(b), and 401(k) assets. This means that the taxable income many individuals will receive from their qualified savings plan will push them into a higher IRMAA tax bracket. The IRMAA tax and its impact on your Social Security benefit will become a reality for many more Americans.

As you consider this grid once again, there are added, unexpected consequences that may arise. For example, when a spouse passes away, the surviving spouse will usually experience a drop in income due to lower Social Security benefits and lower pension benefits. You might logically expect this widow to find herself in a lower IRMAA tax bracket due to the lower income level. However, the resulting drop in income may be more than offset by the higher tax bracket the surviving spouse moves into due to the fact that they must now file as a single. The bottom line could actually result in an increase in Medicare cost for the surviving spouse!

Proper investment and tax planning will significantly reduce the amount of your Part B IRMAA tax. In chapter 3, I will describe strategies to use while accumulating wealth for retirement as well as ideas regarding the distribution of wealth during retirement. As with Medicare Part A, it may be prudent to delay your enrollment in Part B. We will discuss those pros and cons in chapter 4.

Summary of Medicare Parts A and B

- Medicare Part A is funded during working years with a payroll tax deduction. Higher income earners have additional tax on earned income and investment income.

- Medicare Part B is funded upon enrollment with a monthly premium.

- Medicare Part B premiums are increased by an IRMAA tax as your Modified Adjusted Gross Income increases.

- This Medicare Part B premium is deducted from your Social Security benefit.

- Income thresholds at which taxation begins may be drastically reduced.

- Historic inflation rates on these premiums have averaged over 7.0%.

- Accumulating assets in accounts that generate a tax-free cash flow can help you control and even reduce the added taxation on your Medicare Part B premiums.

- Required minimum distributions from qualified accounts (401(k), 403(b), IRA) will push affluent investors into higher Medicare tax brackets.

- If your income has recently dropped, you may benefit from applying for reconsideration. This will base your Medicare B and D tax bracket on current income rather than the standard two-year prior look back.

Medicare Supplement

While Medicare Parts A and B provide a foundation for health care coverage in retirement, there are holes in the coverage that need to be addressed. One method of covering these holes is a Medicare Supplement, more commonly known as a "Medigap" plan. These plans are offered by private insurance companies and will cover many out-of-pocket expenses such as Parts A and B co-payments, coinsurance, and deductibles. The cost and extent of coverage will vary depending on which Medigap plan you purchase. For example, the following list of expenses are covered by a Medigap "Plan F":

- Part A $1,340 deductible

- Part A hospital co-insurance

- Part A skilled care co-insurance for days 21-100

- Part B $183 deductible

- Part B 20% co-insurance

A Medigap Plan F is the most popular choice. It offers the most extensive coverage but usually is the most expensive plan. It is worth exploring a few plans to determine which offers the best value for your particular needs.

There are 10 standardized Medigap plans from which to choose (labeled A, B, C, D, F, G, K, L, M, N). Since these policies are regulated at the state and federal level, each insurance company offers the same basic benefits. For example, each insurance company that offers a Medigap "F" plan must provide coverage for a list of items determined by the regulators. Massachusetts, Minnesota, and Wisconsin have their own standardized Medigap policies. It is important to recognize that the added coverage provided by a Medigap plan is fairly extensive. Of particular note is the 20% coinsurance in Part B that is covered.

Without a Medigap plan, one is exposed to this coinsurance without any limit on liability.

A few things to know about Medigap policies:

- You must have Medicare Part A and Part B in order to purchase a Medigap policy.

- A Medigap policy only covers one person. If you and your spouse both want Medigap coverage, you will each have to buy separate policies.

- For most individuals, the best time to purchase your Medigap policy is during your Medigap open enrollment period. During this period, you cannot be denied coverage and cannot be charged more for pre-existing health conditions.

- Any standardized Medigap policy is guaranteed renewable even if you have health problems. This means the insurance company cannot cancel your Medigap policy as long as you pay the premium.

- You can change Medigap policies, but once you are beyond your open enrollment period you are not guaranteed coverage. Some companies may charge a higher premium, include a waiting period for pre-existing conditions, or even deny coverage.

Medicare Part D

Medicare Part D is a policy that provides prescription drug coverage. A national survey of seniors in the United States reported that more than 80% of people aged 65 or older use at least two medications per week. More than 50% of this population use four or more different medications.[12] One can understand why this is an important part of health care coverage. The primary costs of your coverage include the following.

- Annual deductible (up to $405 in 2018)

- Coinsurance / Co-pay

- Costs in the coverage gap ("donut hole")

- Monthly premiums based on type of plan.

- A tax ("IRMAA") based on your income.

The concept of an annual deductible as well as a co-pay or coinsurance is fairly straightforward. The co-pay may be $10 or $20 each time you order a prescription drug, while coinsurance means you pay a percentage (usually around 25%) of the cost each time you order. Coverage in the coverage gap, also known as the donut hole, is more complicated. The coverage gap begins after you and your drug plan have spent a certain amount for covered drugs. In 2018, once you and your plan have spent $3,750 on covered drugs (including your deductible), you enter the coverage gap. You will now pay 35% of the plan's cost for covered brand-name prescription drugs or 44% of the plan's cost for generic drugs. When your total out-of-pocket costs reach $5,000 you qualify for catastrophic coverage.[13] At that point, you are responsible for a small coinsurance amount or co-payment for covered drugs for the rest of the year. This coverage gap, or donut hole, is scheduled to phase out by 2020 as part of the Patient Protection Affordable Care Act.

Each Part D plan has its own list of covered drugs (both generic and brand name), called a formulary.

This is basically a list of prescription drugs that is preferred by your health plan. Drugs are placed into tiers within the formulary. All plans must cover certain categories of drugs, but which drugs are covered in each category may differ by plan. Generally, a lower tier drug is less expensive than a higher tier drug. Significant factors in determining your health care costs will be your need for medicine and your willingness to use brands that are covered under your plan.

Determining Your Medicare Part D Premium

2016 Single Modified AGI	2016 Joint Modified AGI	2018 Annual Part D Premium*
$85,000 or Less	Less than $170,000	Plan Premium
$85,001 - $107,000	$170,001 - $214,000	+ $156
$107,001 - $133,500	$214,001 - $267,000	+ $403
$133,501 - $160,000	$267,001 - $320,000	+ $650
Above $160,000	Above $320,000	+ $897

As with Medicare Part B, your premium for Part D is increased by the IRMAA tax. Table 2 above should look familiar, as the same income levels are used in Part B and Part D to determine your tax. The Part D premium and IRMAA tax can be paid via a deduction from your Social Security benefit. Since the concept of the IRMAA tax is the same as with your Part B premium, some of the key concepts are similar to the Medicare Part B summary, but are worth repeating.

Summary of Medicare Part D

- Medicare Part D is funded upon enrollment with a monthly premium.

- Medicare Part D premiums are increased by an IRMAA tax as your Modified Adjusted Gross Income increases.

- This Medicare Part D premium is usually taken from your Social Security benefit.

- Income thresholds at which taxation begins may be significantly reduced.

- The full amount of Part D costs is deducted from your Social Security benefit. This is unlike Part B deductions, where the Hold Harmless legislation can limit reductions of Social Security Benefits.

- The combination of the IRMAA tax and rising Parts B and D premiums could result in a flat or even steadily declining Social Security benefit for some retirees.

- Required minimum distributions from qualified accounts (401(k), 403(b), IRA) will push affluent investors into higher Medicare tax brackets.

- If your income has recently dropped, you may benefit from applying for reconsideration. This will base your Medicare B and D tax bracket on current income rather than the standard two-year prior look back.

As with Part B, proper investment and tax planning will significantly reduce the amount of your Part D IRMAA tax. In chapter 3, I will describe strategies to use while accumulating wealth for retirement as well as ideas regarding the distribution of wealth during retirement. As with Medicare Part A, it may be prudent to delay your enrollment in Part D. We will discuss those pros and cons in chapter 4.

Medicare Advantage Plans There is another viable alternative to receiving your Medicare coverage other than the "traditional" coverage plan. Medicare coverage can be obtained through a Medicare Advantage Plan. This is Medicare Part C. These plans are not part of original Medicare but are legally required to offer the same benefits as original Medicare.

These health plans are offered by private companies that contract with Medicare to provide you with all of your Parts A and B benefits. They may be in the form of a Health Maintenance Organization, Preferred Provider Organization, Private Fee-for-Service Plan, Special Needs Plan, or Medicare Medical Savings Account Plan. Most Medicare Advantage Plans also offer prescription drug coverage. If not, you will want to consider purchasing a separate (Part D) prescription drug plan.

The way most of the Advantage Plans work, is to provide you with a network of care providers who have contracted with the Advantage Plan. Each plan will have its own set of specific rules, but the basic concept is to pay less for services provided within the network. Therefore, the obvious first step in analyzing an Advantage Plan is to scrutinize the list of care providers to make sure the physicians and facilities you want to use are on the list. These plans will usually work better in an urban setting, compared to a rural market place, as the universe of care providers within the network is more extensive. As of 2015, approximately 31% of Medicare enrollees choose these plans.[14] The trend over the past few years has seen a modest but steady rise in the Advantage Plan popularity.

Some individuals will purchase an Advantage Plan in order to obtain coverage for items not covered under traditional Medicare. As you would expect, coverage, which is more robust, will usually have a higher cost.

Medicare Advantage Plan

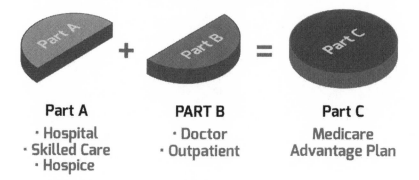

Part A	PART B	Part C
• Hospital	• Doctor	Medicare
• Skilled Care	• Outpatient	Advantage Plan
• Hospice		

Summary of Medicare Advantage Plans

- You must sign up for Medicare Parts A and B in order to purchase an Advantage Plan.

- Since you have Part B, you do not avoid the Part B IRMAA tax.

- You do not avoid the Part D IRMAA tax.

- You cannot have both a Medigap plan and an Advantage Plan.

- You cannot have both a Part D prescription drug plan and an Advantage Plan that offers prescription coverage.

- Some employers will drop your health insurance

coverage if you obtain coverage through an Advantage Plan.

The first two questions from the beginning of the chapter have now been addressed. Medicare, either on its own or in conjunction with other insurance, will provide your health insurance coverage during retirement. I have provided a high-level overview of how the coverage works. The next question to be answered is how much will it cost?

CHAPTER 2

Calculating the Cost

"A nickel ain't worth a dime anymore." —Yogi Berra

Now that I have provided a high-level overview of the various pieces of Medicare, we can begin to obtain an estimate of retirement health care costs. There are a number of factors that will influence this cost. At this point, I will be estimating what I would describe as routine health care expenses. This includes the following:

- Medicare premiums (including IRMAA tax)

- Deductibles

- Co-pays

- Coinsurance

- Medigap

- Medicare Advantage premiums

- Certain uncovered items

I listed certain uncovered items because there is one area of health care cost that is not covered by Medicare and not included in this estimate. It warrants its own discussion of costs and consequences. I am referring to custodial care, the non-medical care required to assist individuals with their basic activities of daily living. Chapter 5 will be devoted to this topic.

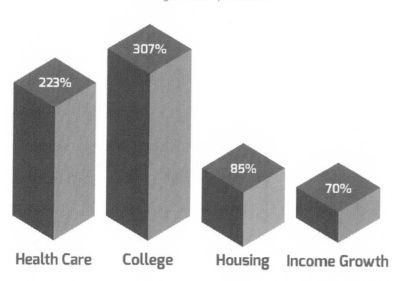

Cost Increase vs. Income Growth 1989-2010*

Washington Post April 3, 2014

In addition to whether or not you need custodial care, there are four primary factors that will impact your health care costs.

The first factor is the inflation rate. The average health

care cost increase from 1989 to 2010 was 223%. To put that in perspective, the average income rose 70% over the same period.[15]

If you assume that health care costs will continue to grow at a similar pace, your cost estimate will be significantly higher than if you assume a historic Consumer Price Index rate.

The Center for Medicare and Medicaid Services projects health care spending to grow at 5.8% per year for the next 10 years.[16] A longer term perspective is offered by Health View Services who report a 5.1% health care inflation rate for the next 20 years.[17] I will use the more conservative 5.1% figure for the illustrations that follow.

The second factor is your level of taxable income. As I described in chapter 1, the IRMAA tax on Medicare Parts B and D is based on your Modified Adjusted Gross Income. The higher your taxable income, the higher your Medicare Parts B and D premiums. I will certainly explore methods of managing your taxable income in a later chapter. To illustrate the importance of this area, I will provide an estimate for individuals at various income levels.

The third factor is your view on the proposed changes to the IRMAA tax. As explained in chapter one, there are proposals well under way that will trigger the tax for millions of additional taxpayers and raise the amount of the tax for those already facing it. Given

Medicare's fiscal challenges described in the 2017 trustee report, I strongly believe these proposals will become a reality. The first move in this direction will be a change to the income grid affecting Medicare Parts B and D premiums in 2018. As you see in the charts below, the income levels triggering the two highest Medicare premiums have been lowered.

Determining Your Medicare Part B Premium

2017 Income Brackets

2015 Single Modified AGI	2015 Joint Modified AGI
$85,000 or less	$170,000 or less
$85,001 - $107,000	$170,001 - $214,000
$107,001 - $160,000	$214,001 - $320,000
$160,001 - $214,000	$320,001 - $428,000
Above $214,000	Above $428,000

2018 Income Brackets

2016 Single Modified AGI	2016 Joint Modified AGI
$85,000 or less	$170,000 or less
$85,001 - $107,000	$170,001 - $214,000
$107,001 - $133,500	$214,001 - $267,000
$133,501 - $160,000	$267,001 - $320,000
Above $160,000	Above $320,000

The last factor is the amount you will need to spend on uncovered items. As it stands today, Medicare does not provide coverage for dental work, hearing aids and vision needs. Your expenditures for prescription drugs will vary based on your willingness or ability to use brands and classes of medicines covered by Medicare.

Estimating your overall costs is, therefore, far from an exact science. It is still, however, wise to use some national averages and make some assumptions based on historical inflation rates in order to obtain a cost estimate. I will look at few different case studies to provide some context.

Scenario number one:

- Married Couple

- Age 65 (2018)

- Taxable Income: $108,000 (Joint MAGI)

- Original Medicare with a Prescription Drug and Medigap Plan (A, B, D, and Medigap)

- Historical Inflation for Plans A, B, D, Medigap, and uncovered items.

- First IRMAA bracket

Scenario Number One
First Year Per Person Cost

Coverage	Per Person First Year Cost
Medicare Part A	$0
Medicare Part B	$1,608
Medicare Part D	$409
Medigap	$2,370
Out of Pocket	$2,385
Total	$6,772

Scenario Number One Annual Costs:
Years One, Ten, and Twenty

Cost	Per Person	Married Couple
Year One Total	$6,772	$13,544
Year Ten Total	$10,595	$21,190
Year Twenty Total	$17,424	$34,848

As you can see in the summary table. This couple should budget over $13,000 for their first year of retirement health care costs. Cumulative costs for a twenty-year retirement period are estimated at $450,000. With life expectancies continuing to lengthen, a more conservative approach would plan for longer than twenty years.

Note that this same illustration can be used to estimate a single person's cost. Assuming that taxable income begins and remains under $85,000, the per person cost column would apply.

Scenario number two: The effect of a higher income (higher IRMAA tax)

- Married Couple

- Age 65 (2018)

- Taxable Income: $285,000 (Joint MAGI)

- Traditional Medicare with a Prescription Drug and Medigap Plan (A, B, D, and Medigap)

- Historical Inflation for A, B, D, Medigap, and uncovered items.

- Fourth IRMAA bracket.

Scenario Number Two
First Year Per Person Cost

Coverage	Per Person First Year Cost
Medicare Part A	$0
Medicare Part B	$4,179
Medicare Part D	$1,059
Medigap[4]	$2,370
Out of Pocket	$2,385
Total	$9,993

Scenario Number Two Annual Costs: Years One, Ten, and Twenty

Cost	Per Person	Married Couple
Year One Total	$9,993	$19,986
Year Ten Total	$15,636	$31,272
Year Twenty Total	$25,713	$51,426

This couple should budget close to $20,000 for their first year of retirement health care costs. Cumulative costs for a twenty-year retirement period are estimated at $667,000. With life expectancies continuing to lengthen, a more conservative approach would plan for longer than twenty years.

Note that this same illustration can be used to estimate a single person's cost. Assuming that taxable income begins and remains between $133,501 and $160,000, the per person cost column would apply.

A word or two on cost estimates for Medicare Advantage Plans. The scenarios all assume coverage with a traditional Medicare. Providing the same type of estimate for those who use an Advantage Plan is much more difficult. These plans vary by a wide degree, not only on the overall premium you pay, but also on how co-pays, coinsurance, and deductibles are structured. Once again, if you choose the Advantage Plan for coverage, you will still have Medicare Parts A and B and all of the associated taxes. If you are reasonably healthy, use an Advantage Plan that provides comparable coverage to Medicare and stay within that plan's network of providers, you usually will lower your overall cost.

Many financial advisors have tools available to estimate the cost of health care in retirement. As you build a financial plan for retirement, inclusion of this cost will provide a superior, comprehensive income plan.

CHAPTER 3

Understanding Tax Control

"Nolan Ryan is pitching much better now that he has his curve ball straightened out." — Joe Garagiola (major league ball player, 1946-1954)

Once you estimate the cost of health care and realize its significance, you will undoubtedly want to know how to best prepare yourself financially. As I stated in the preface, one of my goals in writing this book is not only to help individuals recognize the cost, but take the appropriate action, as it relates to their saving and investment plans. Health care costs are throwing a curve ball into some of the conventional methods of retirement planning. There are a number of tangible steps you should take while accumulating your retirement savings that can put you in a better position to handle health care costs, including their onerous taxation.

The first step is to gain an understanding of which assets will generate taxable income and which ones will not. More specifically, you need to understand what types of income create higher premiums for Medicare Parts B and D.

Your Modified Adjusted Gross Income from two years

ago will determine your current Part B and Part D premiums.[18] In a nutshell, this is line 37 on tax form 1040 (Adjusted Gross Income) plus line 8b (Municipal Bond Income). In order to potentially lower your tax, one must understand what income is counted toward Modified Adjusted Gross and what income is not.

Types of Income Impacting Medicare Part B & Part D Premiums

Income counted toward Medicare B, D IRMAA tax	Income NOT counted toward Medicare B, D IRMAA tax
Wages	Roth IRA
Pension	Roth 401(k)
Social Security (taxable portion)	Annuitized Payments (partial exclusion)
Interest income	HSA (Health Savings Account)
Dividends	401(h) distributions
Capital gains	Certain life insurance distributions
Municipal bond interest	Reverse mortgage
IRA, 401(k), 403(b) withdrawals	

Tax law is rarely without conditions, so it is important to consult with your financial advisor and tax consultant to fully understand the impact of the above listed items.

There are a few items on each side of the list that usually catch people by surprise. The first item is your

Social Security benefit. Not only do many individuals pay ordinary income tax on this benefit, but it can also push you into a higher IRMAA tax rate. The other item that may irk you is the inclusion of "tax-free" municipal bond interest into the Medicare IRMAA tax calculation!

The largest bind comes from many investors who accumulate the majority of their investable assets in qualified plans (IRA, 401(k), 403(b)). The challenge they face is twofold. First, distributions from these accounts are taxed as ordinary income. Second, distributions are mandatory at age 70½ and usually increase with each passing year. If these required distributions bump you into a higher IRMAA tax rate, the result will be tens of thousands of dollars in additional taxes over the course of your retirement. My discussion on Roth IRAs and annuities will help many readers reduce some of this burden.

The obvious consideration as one looks at this list, is to make sure you are accumulating assets in investments that will be able to provide a tax-free cash flow during retirement. Not all of the items in the list above are available to every investor (e.g., your employer may only offer a traditional 401(k), not a Roth 401(k)), nor is each item appropriate for everyone. However, a retirement portfolio that includes a Roth account, Health Savings Account, and an annuity will equip an investor to control taxes.

I will reiterate an item discussed in chapter 1. The

Social Security Administration considers your income from two years ago. If you have experienced a drop in income since 2014, you may be able to lower your tax by having the administration consider your current income. In order to accomplish this, you can apply with a form sent into the Social Security Administration for reconsideration. The most common, acceptable reasons of a loss of income are due to retirement, death of a spouse, or divorce. The entire list consists of the following:[19]

- Marriage

- Divorce/Annulment

- Death of Your Spouse

- Work Stoppage

- Work Reduction

- Loss of Income Producing Property

- Loss of Pension Income

- Employer Settlement Payment

If one of these events affects your income, you can complete form SSA-44 or visit your local Social Security office.

Roth IRA

The Roth IRA should play a meaningful role in most investors' retirement savings plans. The Roth IRA was introduced in 1997 as part of the Tax Payer Relief Act. It was named after Senator William Roth, from Delaware, an advocate of IRA reform.

The basic concept with a Roth IRA is to encourage retirement savings. It does so by providing investors with an account in which the earnings accumulate without taxation. It then allows you to take distributions, usually during your retirement years, without taxation. This means that Roth distributions do not get counted toward your Modified Adjusted Gross Income in determining your IRMAA Medicare tax. You do not receive an income tax deduction for your Roth contribution, but as you are beginning to understand, the freedom from taxes during retirement is a major advantage. There are certainly rules you must follow in order to enjoy this tax-free accumulation and distribution. For example, you must hold the account for five years and be over the age of 591/2 to avoid any penalties on withdrawals. A Roth can be invested in the same list of investments available for a traditional IRA. This list includes the following:[20]

- Mutual funds

- Annuities

- Stocks

- Bonds

- Unit investment trusts

- Exchange traded funds

- Traditional savings accounts

There are primarily three ways to accumulate wealth within a Roth account:

• Contribute to a Roth IRA

• Convert a traditional IRA to a Roth IRA

• Contribute to a Roth 401(k)

Whether or not you are allowed to contribute to a Roth IRA is based on your income (more specifically, your Modified Adjusted Gross Income). If you file a joint return in 2018, and your income is under $189,000 or if you file a single return and your income is under $120,000, you are able to make a full Roth contribution[21]. As your income gets above these levels, the amount you can contribute is lower and goes away completely at certain levels. The IRS chart detailing this information is listed in the table below.

2018 Income Limits to Determine Roth Eligibility

Filing Status	Modified AGI	Contribution
Married, filing jointly or qualified widow(er)	< $189,000	Up to the limit
	≥ $189,000 but < $199,000	A reduced amount
	≥ $199,000	Zero
Single, head of household, or married filing separately	< $120,000	Up to the limit
	≥ $120,000 but < $135,000	A reduced amount
	≥ $135,000	Zero

For those that are able to make a 2018 contribution, the maximum amount is $5,500. If you are age 50 and older you can contribute an extra $1,000 (called a catch-up provision). The contribution limits may rise over the years ahead, based on inflation and government policy.

The Power of Roth IRA

Let us take a look at how powerful a savings tool the Roth IRA can be. Consider a married couple, age 50, who are able to fully fund a Roth ($6,500 per person X 2 = $13,000 in contributions) and continue to do so each year up to age 65. The stock market, as measured by the S&P 500 has averaged an annualized return of 10.9% since 1934.[22] I will use a more conservative 8% return. For simplicity, I will assume that there is no change to the contribution limit.

At age 65, the Roth accounts would each be worth $190,608. Not only has the account enjoyed tax-free compounding over the 15-year period but distributions for this 65-year-old couple are free from federal income tax and Medicare IRMAA tax. Since the distributions are tax-free, there is no requirement minimum distribution at age 70½. Once again:

- Married Couple age 55.

- Invest $13,000 each year into Roth IRAs until age 65.

- 8% return.

- Age 65 combined account values of $381,216.

- Retirement distributions are income tax free and Medicare IRMAA tax free.

• The Power of the Roth 401(k)

For those who are in the workplace and enjoying the perks of employee benefits, you probably have a 401(k) available to encourage retirement savings. According to statistics provided by the U.S. Department of Labor, there are 534,000 401(k) plans, covering more than 94 million participants.[23] Despite the popularity of the traditional 401(k), the Roth 401(k) has not been widely embraced. Even though approximately one half of employers who offer a 401(k) now make the Roth 401(k) available, slightly less than 13% of workers are contributing money to the Roth plan.[24] There are two primary reasons. First, the Roth 401(k) is only a few years old and most people are simply slow to research, embrace, and change to something new. The other explanation is that investors are hungry for any means to lower their current tax liability, and the deductible contributions of a traditional 401(k) are hard to give up.

Regardless of the rational, many investors are missing a tremendous planning opportunity by not using their Roth 401(k). The Roth 401(k) is similar to a traditional 401(k). Contributions are made directly from your paycheck and you may receive some type of matching contribution from your employer. You are provided with a list of approved investment choices for your particular plan. Your money accumulates without current taxation. There are, however, two major differences.

- Your contributions to the Roth 401(k) are not tax-deductible.

- Your distributions from the Roth during retirement are tax-free.

Roth 401(k)s are available to both the largest and to the smallest end of the employer market.

Year 2018 contribution limits for a Roth 401(k) are $18,500 with an age 50+ catch-up provision of $6,000. Let us use an example to illustrate the power of disciplined investing with tax-free growth. We will assume a married couple, age 55, who have just made their last college tuition payment. With their children graduated, they are entering peak retirement saving years, at a time when they are entering their peak earning years. A maximum contribution to a Roth 401(k) each year from age 55 to 65 could create an account valued at $383,314 for each person.

- Married Couple age 55.

- Invest $49,000 each year ($24,500 in each account) into Roth 401(k) until age 65.

- 8% return.

- Age 65 combined account values of $766,628.

- Retirement distributions are income tax free and Medicare IRMAA tax free.

This obviously assumes a robust, disciplined savings program. If the company plan had a matching provision, the accumulation could be even greater. When addressing client groups across the nation, I consistently hear a reluctance to change from the traditional 401(k) to the Roth 401(k) driven by reluctance to forgo a current tax deduction. Most of the information on the traditional versus Roth decision simply asks if you expect to be in a higher tax bracket while you work or when you retire. This guidance very rarely considers the taxation of Medicare during your retirement years. There are many factors in our nation, that point to higher taxes in the years ahead. The projected insolvency of Medicare and resulting tax increase is just one reason why forgoing current tax deductions in order to build a true tax free cash flow with the Roth makes sense.

Roth Conversions

For those who earn too much to make a Roth contribution or do not have a Roth 401(k) available at their workplace, there is yet one more way to accumulate wealth in a Roth account. This method is available to any investor, regardless of income and involvement in employer sponsored plans. Individuals have the ability each year to convert existing IRAs into Roth IRAs. The idea is to pay taxes today on the IRA that you decide to convert, in order to create a tax-free cash flow later, namely in retirement. The reason this can make sense is if you believe that your taxes in retirement, especially when factoring in the taxes that are unique to your retirement years (i.e., Medicare taxes), will be higher than your taxes today. I advise working closely with your financial advisor and accountant to determine if a full or partial conversion of your IRA assets is wise. The details surrounding these conversions go beyond the scope of this chapter. For example, calculating the tax liability on a conversion can be complicated if you have both deductible and non-deductible IRAs. There are methods, however, of isolating your non-deductible IRAs from your deductible IRA's by transferring the latter to your 401(k) plans. Tax liability from a Roth conversion can be offset by tax losses and deductions. Another consideration is whether or not you have funds available to pay the current tax liability. There are even strategies for something called "in plan conversions" that allow you to convert 401(k) dollars into Roth accounts.

The goal of this chapter is not to explain all of the details surrounding the Roth IRA conversion. My point is that most of the popular educational material on retirement planning fails to examine the impact of health care cost on your investment decisions. It, therefore, fails to factor in additional benefits that a Roth provides by its exclusion from the Medicare IRMAA tax.

The Roth IRA should play an important role in your retirement asset accumulation plan. There are multiple ways to accumulate wealth in these fabulous accounts including Roth contributions, Roth 401(k), and Roth conversions. Make sure to explore each of these with your financial advisor and tax professional.

The Heath Savings Account

The Health Savings Account (HSA) provides an excellent means of creating a tax-free cash flow for current and future qualified, medical health care expenses. HSA accounts are used in conjunction with high deductible health insurance plans.

The concept is fairly straightforward. With a high deductible, you pay for more health care items with your own funds before your insurance begins coverage. Since you pay for more items with your own funds, the insurance provider charges a relatively lower premium for coverage. The HSA is an account into which you place money to be used for these non-covered health care expenditures. The primary benefits to the accounts are as follows:

- Personal contributions are fully tax deductible.

- Distributions from the account for qualified health expenditures are tax free.

- The funds in an HSA can be invested.

- Unused funds in the account continue to grow, free from taxes.

- The accounts belong to you even if you change employers or retire.

- Some employers will make a contribution to your account.

Once again, Health Savings accounts are made available to those, and only those, who have an HSA eligible, high deductible health insurance plan. I will refer to these plans as an HDHP. The word "high" is not relative, as the government provides very specific parameters as to which plans qualify as high deductible and HSA eligible. These plans currently serve over 21 million Americans and are growing in popularity as part of a consumer directed movement to deal with rising health care costs.[25] In 2018, a high deductible health plan must have an annual deductible of at least $1,350 for self-only coverage and at least $2,700 for family coverage.[26] Self-only HDHP covers an eligible individual, whereas family HDHP covers an eligible individual and at least one other family member. These plans also carry limits on the maximum out-of-pocket expenditures for families or individuals as well as a few other stipulations. If you withdraw money from the account for something other than a qualified medical expense you will pay a 20% penalty and taxes on the distribution. Once you reach age 65, the 20% penalty is waived. There is no income limit to determine eligibility to contribute to an HSA.

HSAs were established by federal law in December 2003 with the enactment of the Medicare Prescription Drug, Improvement and Modernization Act.

Hopefully, at this point you are wondering how much you can place in an HSA. The 2018 contribution limits are $6,900 for a family plan or $3,450 for a single. Any employer contributions are included in these limits. Those over the age of 55 can contribute an additional $1,000 per year.[27]

I stated that HSA distributions are tax free when used for qualified health care expenditures. The list of items that qualify as health care expenditures is extensive. For a full view you can visit IRS.gov for pages upon pages of these items.

Generally speaking, if the expense is created by a legitimate health care need, it probably is on the list of qualified expenditures. To stimulate some thought on how broad the definition is, consider the following qualified expenditures outside of the usual doctor visits, co-pays, deductibles, and prescription drugs:

- Vision care (eyeglasses, contacts, Lasik surgery)

- Dental work

- Orthopedic shoes

- Vitamins (prescription)

- Hearing aids and batteries

- Therapy equipment

- Long term care insurance premiums (with limits)

- Medicare premiums for Parts A, B, D

- Medicare Advantage premiums

HSA participants can include, in medical expenses,

amounts they pay for special equipment installed in their homes or for improvements if its main purpose is medical care. If the value of the property is not increased by the improvement, the entire cost is a qualified medical expense. Certain improvements made to a home to accommodate a disability do not usually increase the value of the home, and the entire cost can be considered a qualified medical expense. Some examples include the following:

- Constructing entrance or exit ramps.

- Widening doorways at entrances or exits.

- Installing railings or support bars.

- Installing porch lifts and other forms of lifts (elevators are generally deemed to add value to the house).

Since the focus of this book is preparing for health care in retirement, we will consider the tremendous planning tool an HSA can be. The strategy I recommend is as follows:

1. Make the maximum contribution to your HSA account

2. Invest the money.

3. Refrain from using it until retirement.

This will require some discipline. You will enjoy the tax deduction you receive for every dollar placed in the account. This deduction will be particularly appreciated by those who no longer have a 401(k) deduction because of their prudent switch to a Roth 401(K). You will be tempted to take money out of the account to fund your uncovered medical expense with tax-free withdrawals. The ease of making these withdrawals with an HSA provided debit card will require restraint. The result of exercising this discipline can be the creation of a sizable investment account able to fund numerous health care expenditures with tax-free distributions. To illustrate this concept, consider a 50-year-old married couple. This time I will make the following assumptions:

- Contribute the maximum $6,900 to an HSA family account.

- Contribute the additional $2,000 per year starting at age 55 (split the HSA account into two accounts enabling each spouse to contribute $1,000)

- Refrain from making any distributions.

- Invest the money and earn 8%.

For simplicity, I will assume that the contribution limit remains at $6,900. The reality is that the limit will be raised to adjust for inflation, allowing even greater contributions.

At age 65, the HSA account would be valued at over $233,000! In chapter 4, I will discuss the rules and means of continuing contributions beyond age 65 but for now let us assume the couple retires at 65. In addition to paying for routine, uncovered medical expenses with tax-free distributions, they can now consider these same distributions to pay the following:

- Medicare premiums (Parts A, B, D)

- Medicare Advantage premiums

- Long term care insurance premiums (up to a limit)

The account can remain invested, enjoying tax-free growth. If the couple's financial needs change after age 65, and the funds are withdrawn for something other than medical expenses, there are no penalties, just ordinary taxation of amounts withdrawn. When the first spouse passes away, the surviving spouse (assuming he or she was named as the beneficiary) can continue to use the account. As I mentioned at the start of this chapter, HSA accounts have become a core component of the consumer directed movement to deal with rising health care costs. They should, therefore, continue to grow in popularity and use. Once you recognize the ability to put these accounts to use for retirement income planning, they will become a core component of a comprehensive, retirement income plan.

The Annuity

It should be evident at this point that a significant part of planning for health care costs in retirement involves understanding how investments are taxed and utilizing investments that allow you greater control. Annuities that offer tax deferral, tax-favored income, opportunity for growth, and lifetime income guarantees can play a meaningful role in this planning. Annuities come in a variety of shapes and sizes. Financial advisors and the investing public have a wide range of views on these investments from raving fans to major critics. In this section, I will describe the benefits of annuities and how they can be effectively used to position your assets to handle health care costs.

As stated, there are many different types of annuities; variable, fixed, indexed, immediate, and deferred income to name a few. One of the reasons an annuity can be so helpful as it relates to your retirement income, is the control it provides when you take income and pay taxes. The analogy that best communicates this concept is the use of water in your home. When you need water, whether it is for a drink or hot shower, you turn on the faucet for the length of time necessary for the task at hand, and then shut it off. You will be billed only for the amount of water used. You don't leave the shower constantly running and merely jump in each morning as your water bill would be enormous (leaving the waste of resources issue aside). Money invested in an annuity grows tax deferred. This means that while you let the earnings accumulate for later use during retirement years, you do not get taxed. During accumulation, there is no "bill" or 1099 tax document on interest or earnings. When you are ready to make withdrawals from the annuity there are a few different ways to do so. For example, you may decide to take a systematic or periodic cash flow. In this case, you will pay taxes when you decide to take the income, but only on the amount you withdraw.[28] To use the water faucet analogy, you decide how much income you will actually spend, turn on the faucet (make that withdrawal) and pay the tax bill only on that withdrawal.

One effective planning strategy is to use a non-qualified annuity for a portion of your investment monies. This can be particularly useful for investors who reach age 70-1/2 and are forced to take distributions on their "qualified" accounts (primarily IRAs). Since the faucet on your IRA money will be turned on for you at age 70-1/2, it is helpful to have "non-qualified" (non-IRA) money in an annuity, allowing interest and earnings that you are not spending to accumulate without current taxation. In other words, use the taxable cash flow from your IRA and other taxable investments to meet your spending needs and reduce your tax liability (including the IRMAA Medicare tax) by keeping a portion of your non IRA money (especially monies for which you are not spending the earnings) in the annuity.

The bind that some investors face is created by accumulating almost all of their retirement savings in qualified accounts. The required minimum distributions on these accounts at age 70-1/2 push them into higher income and Medicare IRMAA tax brackets. A better approach is to utilize Roth, HSA, and non-qualified annuities along with your qualified savings. This will allow your financial advisor the ability to provide greater after tax income.

Another way to utilize the annuity is to consider taking the income with an annuitized cash flow. In this situation, the annuity company provides you an income stream, usually based on your life expectancy, in which a portion of the payment is taxable and a portion is non taxable. Generally, the income stream is guaranteed for your life and therefore cannot be altered. The benefit, in addition to planning for longevity, is a tax-favored cash flow. Along with the cost of health care, individuals often cite longevity as their top concern when planning for retirement. The list of investment income not subject to the IRMAA tax is fairly short. Annuitization offers partial tax relief and helps address the fear of outliving your income.

As with any investment, annuities have fees, time commitments, and risks to consider before adding them to your portfolio. Money invested in an annuity is usually money you will not need until age 59-1/2 or later. Levels of risk can be dialed up or down depending on your choice of fixed rate, index, or variable. In addition to the annuitized payment plan described in this section, many annuities offer flexible withdrawal plans with lifetime guarantees. The tax treatment will vary based on which type of withdrawal method you choose. Take the time to review the benefits and costs with your financial advisor.

Additional Sources

I have spent some time and provided some detail on the most common steps individuals can take to best position their retirement savings to deal with health care costs. These core strategies include the Roth, the HSA, and annuity. There are a few other ideas worth mentioning. They fall into what I would describe as niche ideas, meaning the opportunity to take advantage of these ideas is not as widely available as the core strategies. If you are able to utilize them, however, they can be quite beneficial and therefore worthy of at least a short overview.

401(h)

The first of these ideas is a 401(h) plan for small business owners. The 401(h) is an account, similar to an HSA, designed to facilitate savings for health care expenditures. It is available to business owners who have a defined benefit pension plan. This can be a traditional defined benefit pension or even a cash balance plan. The key is that a 401(h) can only work in conjunction with one of these plans, meaning it cannot stand alone or cannot be tied to a defined contribution plan (i.e. Profit Sharing, 401(k), SEPP). Small business owners use their defined benefit plan in order to make substantial retirement savings in the years leading into retirement. A properly structured defined benefit plan will allow contributions that are substantially higher than a defined contribution plan. The business owner must make a strong financial commitment in order to fund the plan. The profile, therefore, is usually a very successful business owner in his or her late forties to early sixties. The 401(h) account allows a portion (up to 25%) of the monies that otherwise would flow into the investment accounts of the pension to flow into an investment account designated for health care expenditures. The contributions are tax deductible, grow tax free, and can be distributed for health care expenditures tax free. When fully funding this type of plan, one can contribute tens of thousands of dollars each year into the 401(h).[29]

VEBA / Life Insurance / Reverse Mortgages

VEBA stands for Voluntary Employees' Beneficiary Association. These tax-exempt associations provide a means for employers and employees to fund various health related benefits. They are most commonly used by nonprofit organizations but are occasionally found in the profit sector as well. The specific programs and rules may vary for each VEBA. If your employer or employee association makes a VEBA available it is worth considering. Many offer an account in which both the employer and employee contribute dollars to fund health expenditures. Contributions are tax deductible, earnings grow tax free, and distributions for health expenditures are tax free.[30]

Hopefully you can see a theme developing. Equipping yourself to fund health care costs is in large part tied to finding the savings and investment programs that provide meaningful tax advantages to do so. At the beginning of the chapter, I provided a list of types of income that are counted toward the Medicare IRMAA tax and a list of types of income that are not. There are two sources of income on the list that I have not described. The first are the loans available from certain types of permanent life insurance policies. I point this out because we have learned that "tax free" does not always mean tax free. For example, tax-free municipal bond income is not tax free when it comes to determining your Medicare IRMAA tax bracket. With permanent life insurance policies, the tax-free loans you make against the policy are indeed tax free. In other words, they do not count as income in determining your Medicare IRMAA tax. There are varying opinions within the financial planning community on the wisdom of using life insurance as an investment product and source of retirement income. The ability to withdraw the cash value without impacting your IRMAA tax is a strong point in favor of owning permanent life policies and one that most critics do not consider. If you own a permanent life policy, make sure your financial advisor is aware of the policy. They may decide, in certain situations to utilize the tax-free loan feature.

The last source of tax-free income I will discuss is the income created from a reverse mortgage. The advantages and limitations of taking out a reverse mortgage on your property are well beyond the scope of this book. In its simplest form, a reverse mortgage is a product that allows you to convert part of the equity in your home into cash without having to sell your home. You receive money from the lender, and generally do not have to pay it back for as long as you live in your home. The loan is repaid when you die, sell your home, or when your home is no longer your primary residence. They are available to individuals age 62 or older. The proceeds of a reverse mortgage generally are tax free. A cash flow from a reverse mortgage will not count toward your Medicare IRMAA tax bracket.

CHAPTER 4

Timing Your Medicare Enrollment

"You don't have to swing hard to hit a home run. If you got the timing, it'll go." — Yogi Berra

The usual age for enrollment in Medicare is age 65. Many individuals, however, are realizing that delaying enrollment may be a prudent plan. In this chapter, I will explore the following points:

- The advantages of deferring some or all of your Medicare enrollment.

- The rules one must follow in order to defer.

Medicare has substantial costs. Some of the costs include the following:

- Medicare Part B premiums. The premium includes a tax for those with higher incomes. Part B premiums, for an individual, range between $1,608 and $5,143 per year in 2018.[31]

- Your 2018 Part D premium. This premium can be increased by up to $897 per year, based on your income.[32]

- Medigap or Medicare Advantage plans costs thousands of dollars per year.

Medicare coverage is, overall, extensive. If, however, you have comprehensive coverage provided by an employer or even your spouse's employer, it may be prudent to defer some or all of your Medicare enrollment to simply defer the above-mentioned costs.

Let us look at two fairly common situations in order to work through the key considerations when deferring Medicare enrollment.

Scenario number one:

You are still working or your spouse is still working and you wish to delay Medicare enrollment. In order to defer Medicare in its entirety, one must do the following:

- Defer enrollment in Social Security.

- Have appropriate health insurance coverage from your employer or your spouse's employer, of 20 or more employees.

Unfortunately, the smaller end of the employee market is boxed out of this opportunity. For those who do meet these two qualifications, Medicare in its entirety or in part can be deferred each year in which you have appropriate company provided coverage. This insurance coverage must be at least as extensive as Medicare coverages. It is advisable to obtain written documentation, each year, from your employer's benefits department stating that your insurance coverage is creditable. "Creditable" is a Medicare term, primarily referring to Medicare Part D, which basically states that the coverage is extensive enough to work in lieu of Medicare.[33] When you enroll in Medicare at a later date, you will need to show that you had appropriate coverage from your employer in order to avoid late enrollment penalties.

If you have not started your Social Security benefit and have the company provided insurance described, you can delay Medicare Parts A and B. Since Part D is not mandatory, anyone can defer or decline enrollment. If you need Part D at a later point, you will want to have the documentation showing your creditable coverage to avoid a Part D late enrollment penalty.

Medigap plans are also not mandatory and therefore can be deferred or declined. Medigap policies are best purchased during what is called an open enrollment period. For those who retire and are age 65 or older there is an open enrollment period with guaranteed issue rights called Medigap Protection. This means you cannot be denied a policy and you cannot be charged more for it. If you apply for a Medigap policy outside of a normal enrollment period the gap company can deny coverage but most do not. Some may impose a 6-month waiting period on preexisting conditions.

Let me summarize this situation. You or your spouse are working for a company with 20 or more employees who provides insurance coverage and you have not commenced your Social Security benefits. You are able to defer Medicare Parts A, B, D, and Medigap enrollment. The annual savings in premiums and taxes could be thousands of dollars. When you do retire and wish to enroll, you will be given special enrollment periods to obtain your coverage. These special enrollment periods allow you to sign up for Medicare without late enrollment penalties.

You may be wondering if there is any benefit to delaying enrollment in Medicare Part A since it does not carry a cost for most individuals. The savings in delaying Parts B, D, and the Medigap are obvious as these parts carry meaningful costs. The primary reason to defer Part A is to continue funding your Health Savings Account (HSA). As described in chapter 3, an HSA is an account offered in conjunction with a high deductible health insurance plan. The account allows you to contribute funds and take a full tax deduction for the contribution. The earnings on the funds grow tax free and can be distributed free of taxes for a broad range of health care expenditures. As I illustrated, consistently funding an HSA is one of the best ways to prepare yourself for retirement health care costs. Delaying enrollment in Medicare, allows you to continue to fund your HSA. Once an individual enrolls in Medicare A or B, he or she is no longer eligible to contribute to an HSA. If HSA accounts are not part of your strategy, you can enroll in Part A and defer B, D, and Medigap.

Scenario number two:

You need the income from your Social Security benefits but would like to defer the costs of Medicare.

For those who wish to enroll in Social Security, it is important to realize that once you enroll in Social Security, you have enrolled in Medicare Part A. You can, however, decline Part B, assuming once again you have appropriate coverage. It may be smart to decline Part B, as it has a large cost for upper income earners. As in the first scenario, you will need:

- Appropriate health insurance coverage from your employer or your spouse's employer, of 20 or more employees.

This coverage must be at least as extensive as Medicare coverage. By deferring Part B as well as Part D and Medigap, your savings should be thousands of dollars per year.

If you are already collecting Social Security you will be automatically enrolled in both Medicare Parts A and B. You can turn down Part B, but you will need to send back the Medicare card you received in the mail with the form you received stating that you do not want Part B. You will receive a new Medicare card in the mail that does not have Part B on it. Once again, when you do retire, you will have special open enrollment for Parts B, D, and Medigap.

It is worth providing some level of detail on special enrollment periods. These periods of time vary, depending on which part of Medicare you have deferred. For example, you have an 8-month Special Enrollment Period to sign up for Part A and/or Part B that begins the month after your employment ends or the group health insurance ends, whichever happens first.[34] Many employees elect to COBRA their insurance for 18 months upon retirement. Note that the special enrollment period begins when you retire, not at the end of your COBRA period.

The penalties for missing your special enrollment, and thereby enrolling late, are significant. The Medicare Part B penalty is an increase in your Part B premium. The premium is increased 10 percent for each year that you are late enrolling.[35] For example, if you are three years late in enrolling, you will see a 30% increase in your Part B premium each year for as long as you pay for Part B. If you delay enrolling because you have employer coverage, you're given a special enrollment when you do retire that enables you to completely avoid the penalty.

The Part D penalty, even though Part D is not mandatory, is an increase in your monthly prescription drug premium. For each month you did not have creditable coverage, the penalty is one percent. The penalty is cumulative and lasts for as long as you purchase Part D coverage.[36] For example, 24 months without coverage would mean a 24 percent increase in your Part D premium. If you show Medicare the reason you delayed was because you had creditable coverage from your employer, you avoid the penalty. It is a good idea to get something in writing from your employer each year stating you had creditable coverage.

Although the trend in our nation is to delay retirement and continue working, there are certainly many workers stepping away from employment prior to age 65, the magic age to enroll in Medicare. This means if you are thinking about retiring before age 65 you will need to build the funds into your financial plan to pay for private insurance unless you are covered by your spouse's company plan. Three exceptions which may allow you to enroll in Medicare prior to age 65 include a Social Security disability, end stage renal disease, and Lou Gehrig's disease.[37]

Most retirees put considerable time in planning out the optimal time to commence their Social Security benefit. This is time well spent, as the decision will directly impact the amount of your retirement income. This decision, however, should not be made in a vacuum but should be coordinated with the optimal time to enroll in Medicare. This coordination and timing should be a staple component of your comprehensive retirement income plan. Many financial advisors have tools to help estimate the cost of health care and to assist with your Social Security decision.

CHAPTER 5

Custodial Care

"Things could be worse. Suppose your errors were counted and published every day, like those of a baseball player." — Author Unknown

The Medicare coverage described in chapter 1 is extensive but there is one area that is not covered that must be addressed in every financial plan. It can be an enormously expensive area, with financial, emotional, and physical consequences. I am referring to custodial care. This is the non-medical care provided to individuals to assist them with their normal, activities of daily living. Failing to think through a course of action in this area can be the largest error one can make within their financial plan.

Some clarification on this issue is helpful. The purpose of this book is not to provide great detail on which procedures and medicines are covered by Medicare. Providing some level of detail will, however, enable you to better plan for custodial care. It is helpful to make a distinction between skilled care and custodial care. Medicare makes this distinction in terms of who provides the care. To simplify, skilled care is medical care provided by skilled, medical specialists (i.e., doctors, nurses, and occupational therapists). Skilled care is covered by Medicare by the various methods described in chapter 1. Custodial care is care for non-medical activities of daily living (bathing, dressing, eating, mobility, toileting, and grooming) provided by non-medical personnel. This is the type of care that is generally not covered by Medicare. I say generally because there certainly can be overlap with these two types of care. If you receive custodial care from skilled care personnel as part of an overall medical treatment plan, Medicare will provide payment. For example, you may need help with activities of daily living from a nurse while he or she provides medical treatment.

Hospice care, which is the care provided to keep one comfortable in an end of life setting is covered by Medicare.

The main items to understand, as they relate to custodial care are the following:

- Medicare will not pay for custodial care in the absence of a skilled care plan.

- Medicare is not a long term funding solution for custodial care needs.

The need for custodial care is often created by a medical condition that causes a physical or cognitive impairment. Many Americans are experiencing this first hand as our population ages. Many more are experiencing it by providing care for a spouse, parent, or grandparent. There is an abundance of written material on this subject. Most of it provides vast statistical data regarding life expectancy, probability charts on the likelihood of needing care, breakdowns by gender, costs of care, average length of care, and much more. I will provide a few, pertinent numbers to set the stage for this important discussion, but ask you to recognize that the emotional and physical consequences of not properly planning for this event are every bit as important as the financial portion of this topic. In fact, proper financial planning for custodial care usually takes place as a result of the personal side of this discussion.

The foundation of proper planning for custodial care begins with the following facts:

- Most people will need some level of custodial care at some point in their life.

- Most people will receive this care at home, although a meaningful number will require care in a formal facility for at least a portion of this time.

- Custodial care is expensive.

- Custodial care has enormous practical, physical, and emotional consequences on family members who provide this care.

In order to begin the planning process for custodial care, one must begin with a simple acknowledgment. You may need this type of care at some point. I point this out because most people ignore this reality by acknowledging that most people will need custodial care while denying that they will be one of them. It is a simple belief that it will not happen to them. If we can at least acknowledge it is a possibility, we can move on to discuss the consequences. An example of this thought process and resulting action can be found with a few financial products. Life insurance, for example, is designed to provide financial protection to our loved ones in the unlikely event we die a premature death. Most people do not believe that they will die a premature death and yet most people do take out a life insurance policy. Why? The reason is twofold. There is an acknowledgment that even though it is unlikely and unexpected, it could happen. More importantly, there is a consideration of the consequences on those whom you love if it were to take place.

Disability insurance gives us another example. This insurance provides financial protection, in the form of an income, in the unlikely event that we become permanently or partially disabled during our working years. Most people do not expect to become disabled but plenty make sure they have a disability insurance policy. Once again, the reasoning is the same with an acknowledgment that even though a disability is unlikely, it could happen. What follows is a consideration of the consequences on those whom you love if it were to take place.

To understand the consequences of custodial care, one

must think through who provides this care. According to the U.S Department of Health and Human Services, most Americans will be informal caregivers at some point during their lives. During any given year, there are more than 44 million Americans (21% of the adult population) who provide unpaid care to an elderly or disabled person 18 years or older.

- Sixty-one percent of caregivers are women.

- Most caregivers are middle aged.

- Thirteen percent of caregivers are aged 65 years and older.

- Fifty-nine percent of informal caregivers have jobs in addition to caring for another person.[38]

The most common picture that is created is one of a wife, caring for her aging husband or a daughter caring for her widowed mother. The work of caregiving is often described as meaningful, rewarding, and fulfilling but also demanding and difficult. The consequences to the caregiver may include the following:

- Stress, fatigue, anger, depression

- Disruption of the caregiver's life and responsibilities

- Friction between siblings caring for a parent

- Illness for the caregiver

- Financial sacrifice

- Guilt (Is the level of care I provide good enough?)

This is a daunting and depressing list. The reality is that when we honestly consider the consequences to our loved ones, we should take action and put a plan in place to minimize the chance of these occurrences. Since the purpose of this book is to focus on the convergence of health care and financial planning, I will transition to the importance of creating a source of income to alleviate some of these consequences. This is not to say that the solution to these challenges is purely financial, but having a solid source of income can be a massive relief to the caregiver. The first thing it allows is for the caregiver to hire professional assistance for the task at hand. This may be hiring someone to provide all of the care or some portion of it. The dynamic that takes place when a source of income is available is that the family member is no longer providing the care (at least not in its entirety). He or she is overseeing the care. This is a huge difference. In some situations, the level of care required is beyond the scope of what can be provided at home by family or even professional caregivers. This necessitates the placement of a loved one in a nursing home. If a nursing home is the best, or even the only option, having a source of income to pay for the facility is every bit as important.

The question you should be asking at this point is how to have your investment plan ready to create this income if and when it is needed. We have already established that Medicare, absent any medical skilled care needs, will not fund custodial care. What about Medicaid? Medicaid is a government insurance program for those whose income and assets are insufficient to pay for health care. It is jointly funded by the state and federal governments and managed by the states. Each state has broad leeway to determine eligibility. The concept is one of a safety net, for those who do not have sufficient savings and income to pay for care. This also applies to those who have spent their savings down to a minimal level, thus no longer having the ability to pay for care. If you plan on maintaining any meaningful level of assets during retirement, Medicaid is not the solution to funding custodial care.

One development worthy of mention is the enforcement of filial laws as they relate to Medicaid payment. The term filial is defined as relating to, or befitting a son or daughter. There are 30 states that have various and differing rules in their legislatures regarding a son or daughter's obligation to financially provide for a parent's financial needs.[39] These laws have rarely been enforced, but in 2012 a nursing home won a case in the Pennsylvania courts, in which one of three children was mandated to pay his mother's $93,000 nursing home bill after she had left the country to be cared for by family members in Greece.[40] The court did not find that the adult son had engaged in any fraudulent transfers to divert or hide his mother's assets. They simply confirmed Pennsylvania's filial law stating that children can be liable for these types of debts. The safety net of Medicaid may not be as tight as we once believed.

If Medicare and Medicaid are not the solution, should you simply use your existing savings and investment portfolio to generate income for custodial care? This strategy can work, but has limitations that make it close to impossible for most Americans. One reason is the sheer magnitude of the cost. A home health aid will cost approximately $23 per hour. The national average for just one year in a nursing home with a private room is over $102,930.[41] The average length of a stay in the nursing home is 2.4 years[42], but there is certainly no guarantee that planning for that length will be sufficient. Layering this level of expense on most Americans' retirement savings is simply not an option. If you do have a large retirement nest egg, there are still a few items to consider:

- Taxes: Do the assets carry a low cost basis? If so, how much will be paid to the IRS before you can determine funds available for custodial care? Is the largest portion of your wealth in qualified money (401(k), 403(b), IRA)? If so, withdrawals are taxed as ordinary income and may push you into a high tax bracket.

- Liquidity: Are your assets invested in a way that

enables a significant cash flow? For example, real estate investments may not be readily available.

- Timing of your need: Interest rates and stock market movements do not take into consideration the time of your withdrawals. If you need the cash flow at a time of a major stock market downturn, the negative impact on the capital you are depending on can be dramatic.

- Legacy assets: Is the asset you are depleting one you would rather leave as an inheritance?

- Current income needs: Are the assets you are using to fund custodial care needed to fund existing retirement income needs?

This leads us to a discussion on the optimal ways to prepare for custodial care funding. I will consider the major types of products designed to create income for custodial care needs.

Traditional long term care insurance in many ways remains an ideal solution. This insurance can create a cash flow to pay for things such as custodial care expenses either at home or in a nursing home, adult day care, and even care coordination. In order to obtain a policy, you must go through underwriting and be accepted by the insurance company. The policy requires an annual or monthly premium. In return for this premium, the insurance will pay out a stated amount for a stated period of time in the event you cannot perform two out of six activities of daily living or in the event you have a cognitive impairment. The amount that is paid will usually be described as a maximum daily benefit. Policies are regulated by individual states as well as the National Association of Insurance Commissioners. This means all long term care policies must meet minimum standards. They will, however, vary based on factors such as the amount of benefit payable, whether or not you want inflation protection with the benefit, the length of time the benefit will pay, the amount of time you must wait before a policy will pay, as well as other factors. The income created from the policies is tax free in most situations. Your financial advisor can customize a proposal for your consideration based on individual circumstances.

Long term care insurance is expensive primarily due to the simple fact that custodial care is expensive. Recent factors have caused many annual, double digit rate increases on existing policies. When obtaining new coverage, the older you are, the more expensive the policy becomes and the harder it may be to qualify by meeting the underwriting requirements. The average age of someone who purchases a policy is 56. This has dropped meaningfully when you consider the average age was 61 in 2005 and 68 back in 1998.[43] Most advisors recommend purchasing this insurance between your late forties and mid-sixties.

The practical benefit of this insurance is the income created for custodial care. The ultimate benefit is to the caregiver. This insurance is creating peace of mind, better health, and quality of life by allowing your loved ones to supervise a plan for care rather than deliver it.

There are additional solutions available to meet custodial care needs. There has been significant growth in hybrid policies. Despite the clunky name, these policies can be an attractive solution. The name hybrid is used because these products combine features of long term care insurance with other forms of insurance. The most popular will link a long term care benefit to a life insurance policy. Policies can be funded with a lump sum or in some cases over a period of time. The policy will create a stated amount of income, payable for a fixed period of time. Income will usually be free from income tax. In addition, if the policy is not needed for custodial care, a life insurance death benefit will pay out upon the death of the owner. These policies also have an actual account value, meaning some or even all of your contributions can be withdrawn in the event your needs change and you do not mind losing the custodial care coverage. Consumers particularly like this feature when they have concerns about paying annual premiums for traditional long term care insurance with the possibility of never needing the insurance. Some level of underwriting is usually required but is less stringent than applying for traditional long term care coverage. The average purchaser invests over $100,000 in this type of product[44] in order to create a meaningful amount of custodial care coverage. The policy can be funded in one lump sum or with some products, over a period of years (2-10 is typical). If you have a large enough portfolio to consider a hybrid policy, the added flexibility may make it a good choice.

Continuing with the linked products, there is a solution that links a long term care benefit to a fixed annuity. The concept here is to maintain the benefits of tax-deferred accumulation provided by an annuity, while also creating an income tax-free cash flow available to fund custodial care needs. While some of the principle protection offered by a fixed annuity may be sacrificed, there are liquidity provisions to allow you to pull money out if your needs change. Funding can come not only from your own savings and investment dollars but also from exchanging and existing annuity into an annuity linked solution. Underwriting, once again, is simplified, making it less difficult than obtaining approval for traditional long term care coverage.

Lastly, there continues to be innovation with traditional life insurance products. Some carriers will allow you to access your death benefit, in the form of either a lump sum or income stream, in the event of a custodial care need. The requirements and details surrounding these benefits will vary from one insurance provider to another. It is not a comprehensive solution to custodial care funding but can complement coverage or be used as a starting point to your overall strategy. The rules allowing access to your funds from life insurance policies and annuities for long term care needs are usually different than traditional and hybrid long term care insurance. Typically, one must be terminally ill in order to trigger a distribution from a life or annuity product.

As you would expect, there are many considerations to make when evaluating these choices. Your financial advisor can explain the fees, taxes, time commitments, risks, and other detail involved with each of these solutions. The mistake most people make is not choosing the wrong solution but choosing to ignore the need altogether. I hope you will consider that the people most impacted by the failure to have a plan are the ones you love the most and that this realization will cause you to implement a solution into your overall financial plan.

CHAPTER 6

Play Ball

"I've only been doing this fifty-four years. With a little experience, I might get better." — Harry Caray (professional baseball broadcaster, 1945-1997)

Many Americans, as they head into retirement, hold their financial assets with multiple financial institutions. There are many reasons leading to this situation. Over the course of a career most individuals work for multiple employers, each providing their own retirement plan. When one employment period ends, a decision is made to keep the financial assets at the employer or roll them over to a particular custodian. Three or four employers lead to three or four separate and distinct accounts.

Regarding traditional savings accounts, in an effort to squeak out a few extra percentage points of yield, savers often open accounts at multiple banks. Once again, as assets mature and interest rate promotions shift, it is easy to spread these accounts across several financial institutions.

Investment accounts were spread out as you decided to work with multiple financial advisors based on changes in your residence or based on the advisors' various expertise with particular investments. Perhaps you have a family member who, at some point was in the insurance business and still holds your life insurance policies. It is not usually a conscious effort, but many of us at some point realize that quarterly statements and annual tax reporting are flowing in from three, four, or five different financial companies.

One of the problems created when assets are held with multiple institutions or multiple advisors, is that it becomes extremely difficult to create a cohesive asset allocation strategy. Determining the optimal and appropriate mix of equity, fixed income, alternatives, real estate, domestic, and international investments becomes next to impossible. Even creating a starting point for the investment plan becomes overwhelming, as one cannot get a comprehensive picture of current holdings. Updating these allocations throughout retirement is important as the appropriate allocation to growth oriented investments, so critical with rising health care costs, must be effectively calculated and revisited.

Custodial care planning is more effective when implemented within the context of all of your insurance and investment positions. As I described in chapter 5, custodial care planning is really income planning. Income from a long term care product will impact how your other assets are allocated.

When the added complexities of health care costs are factored in, the need to consolidate all of one's assets with a single, competent advisor becomes clear. This advisor should have a working relationship with your tax professional, allowing them to create the necessary mix of taxable, tax free, and tax deferred solutions. It will allow the advisor to coordinate the timing of withdrawals from these accounts.

Many investors do consolidate their assets as they make a transition from accumulating assets to creating income from these assets. While this is prudent, the optimal planning for health care in retirement should begin well in advance of this transition. Many of the strategies I have described, such as choosing a Roth 401(k) over a traditional 401(k), choosing a Roth IRA over a traditional IRA, and investing assets into an HSA account, must be implemented many years ahead of the commencement of your retirement income. Late is better than never, but consolidating assets with one advisor early, while there is time to implement these ideas and allow the strategies time to work, is clearly ideal.

End Notes:

[1] Health and Retirement: Planning for the Great Unknown; A Merrill Lynch study conducted in partnership with Age Wave; 2014.

[2] The annual Mercer Workplace Survey of retirement plan participants June 2013.

[3] The annual Mercer Workplace Survey of retirement plan participants June 2013.

[4] 2017 Annual Report of the Boards of Trustees of the Federal Hospital Insurance and Federal Supplementary Medical Insurance Trust Funds.

[5] https://www.medicare.gov/your-medicare-costs/part-a-costs/part-a-costs.html

[6] https://www.irs.gov/newsroom/net-investment-income-tax-faqs

[7] https://www.medicare.gov/your-medicare-costs/part-a-costs/part-a-costs.html

[8] https://www.medicare.gov/your-medicare-costs/part-b-costs/part-b-costs.html

[9] https://fas.org/sgp/crs/misc/R40082.pdf

[10] 2017 Annual Report of the Boards of Trustees of the Federal Hospital Insurance and Federal Supplementary Medical Insurance Trust Funds.

[11] Bipartisan Policy Center April 2013: A Bipartisan Rx for Patient-Centered Care and System-Wide Cost Containment.

[12] https://blog.medicarerights.org/aarp-survey-highlights-prescription-drug-use-among-older-adults/

[13] https://www.medicare.gov/part-d/costs/part-d-costs.html

[14] http://kff.org/medicare/state-indicator/enrollees-as-a-of-total-medicare-population/

[15] Washington Post; April 3, 2014.

[16] https://www.cms.gov/research-statistics-data-and-systems/statistics-trends-and-reports/nationalhealthexpenddata/nationalhealthaccountsprojected.html

[17] Health View Services 2016 Retirement Health Care Costs Data Report

[18] https://www.medicare.gov/your-medicare-costs/part-b-costs/part-b-costs.html

[19] https://www.ssa.gov/forms/ssa-44.pdf

[20] https://www.irs.gov/retirement-plans/retirement-plans-faqs-regarding-iras-investments

[21] https://www.irs.gov/retirement-plans/plan-participant-employee/retirement-topics-ira-contribution-limits

[22] ICA Guide 2015 edition; page 20

[23] https://www.americanbenefitscouncil.org/pub/?id=e613e1b6%2Df57b%2D1368%2Dc1fb%2D966598903769

[24] http://www.pionline.com/article/20170904/PRINT/170909964/lack-of-education-cited-in-low-takeup-of-roth-plan-option

[25] http://www.devenir.com/research/2017-midyear-devenir-hsa-research-report/

[26] https://www.irs.gov/publications/p969/ar02.html#en_US_2014_publink1000204025

[27] https://www.irs.gov/publications/p969/ar02.html#en_US_2014_publink1000204025

[28] http://www.irionline.org/government-affairs/annuities-regulation-industry-information/taxation-of-annuities

[29] https://www.irs.gov/pub/irs-tege/chap801.pdf

[30] https://www.irs.gov/pub/irs-tege/eotopico82.pdf

[31] https://www.medicare.gov/your-medicare-costs/part-b-costs/part-b-costs.html

[32] https://www.medicare.gov/part-d/costs/part-d-costs.html

[33] https://www.medicare.gov/forms-help-and-resources/mail-about-medicare/notice-of-creditable-coverage.html

[34] https://www.medicare.gov/sign-up-change-plans/get-parts-a-and-b/when-sign-up-parts-a-and-b/when-sign-up-parts-a-and-b.html

[35] http://www.medicareinteractive.org/page2.php?topic=counselor&page=script&script_id=316

[36] https://www.medicare.gov/part-d/costs/penalty/part-d-late-enrollment-penalty.html

[37] https://medicare.com/original-medicare/can-i-get-medicare-if-i-am-under-age-65/

[38] https://www.caregiver.org/women-and-caregiving-facts-and-figures

[39] https://www.medicalalertadvice.com/articles/does-state-law-require-you-to-support-you-aging-parent/

[40] Health Care & Retirement Corporation of America v. Pittas (Pa. Super. Ct., No. 536 EDA 2011, May 7, 2012).

[41] https://whatcarecosts.com/Sponsor#/

[42] https://pocketsense.com/the-average-length-of-stay-in-a-skilled-nursing-facility-12386771.html

[43] AHIP (America's Health Insurance Plans) Findings: Who Buys Long Term Care Insurance 2010

[44] https://www.wsj.com/articles/how-to-size-up-hybrid-long-term-care-policies-1399162059